STO

Dear Parent:

Your child's love of reading starts here!

Every child learns to read in a different way and at his or her own speed. You can help your young reader improve and become more confident by encouraging his or her own interests and abilities. You can also guide your child's spiritual development by reading stories with biblical values and Bible stories, like I Can Read! books published by Zonderkidz. From books your child reads with you to the first books he or she reads alone, there are I Can Read! books for every stage of reading:

SHARED READING

Basic language, word repetition, and whimsical illustrations, ideal for sharing with your emergent reader.

BEGINNING READING

Short sentences, familiar words, and simple concepts for children eager to read on their own.

READING WITH HELP

Engaging stories, longer sentences, and language play for developing readers.

READING ALONE

Complex plots, challenging vocabulary, and high-interest topics for the independent reader.

ADVANCED READING

Short paragraphs, chapters, and exciting themes for the perfect bridge to chapter books.

I Can Read! books have introduced children to the joy of reading since 1957. Featuring award-winning authors and illustrators and a fabulous cast of beloved characters, I Can Read! books set the standard for beginning readers.

A lifetime of discovery begins with the magical words **"I Can Read!"**

Visit www.icanread.com for information on enriching your child's reading experience.
Visit www.zonderkidz.com for more Zonderkidz I Can Read! titles.

There were shepherds living out in the fields nearby.
It was night, and they were looking after their sheep.
An angel of the Lord appeared to them. And the glory of the
Lord shone around them. They were terrified. But the angel
said to them, "Do not be afraid. I bring you good news of
great joy. It is for all the people. Today in the town of David
a Savior has been born to you. He is Christ the Lord."
—*Luke 2:8–11*

ZONDERKIDZ

Baby Jesus Is Born
Copyright © 2009 by Mission City Press. All Rights Reserved.
All Beginner's Bible copyrights and trademarks (including art, text, characters, etc.)
are owned by Mission City Press and licensed by Zondervan of Grand Rapids,
Michigan.

Requests for information should be addressed to:

Zondervan, *Grand Rapids, Michigan 49530*

Library of Congress Cataloging-in-Publication Data
Jesus is born / illustrated by Kelly Pulley.
　　　　p. cm.
　　　　ISBN 978-0-310-71780-5 (softcover)
　　　　1. Jesus Christ—Nativity—Juvenile literature. I. Pulley, Kelly.
　　BT315.3.J45 2009
　　232.92—dc22   2008049732

Editor: *Mary Hassinger*
Art direction: *Jody Langley*

Printed in China

09 10 11 12 13 14 • 5 4 3 2 1

Baby Jesus Is Born

pictures by Kelly Pulley

There was a girl
named Mary.
She loved God very much.

Mary knew a man called Joseph.
They were going to
be married soon.

One day, God sent an
angel to Mary.

The angel said,

"You will have a baby boy.

He is God's Son."

Mary asked, "How can it be?
I am not married yet."

The angel said to Mary,
"God can do anything!"

Joseph and Mary got married.
They loved God's Son
growing in Mary's tummy.

Joseph and Mary had to go
on a long trip.
They went to Bethlehem.
It was far away.

Mary and Joseph needed
a place to stay.
Mary was going to have
the baby soon!

But there were no rooms left.
A man said, "You can sleep in
my stable."

That night, a baby boy
was born.
The baby was Jesus!

Mary wrapped Jesus in cloths.

She put him in a manger.

Angels came to some shepherds.

An angel said, "Good news!

A Savior was born today!"

The shepherds went to see
Baby Jesus.

The shepherds were so happy.

They shouted, "Jesus is born!

He is our Savior!"

Some time later,
wise men saw a new star.
It meant a baby king
was born.

The wise men followed the star.
On their way, they stopped
to see King Herod.

The wise men wanted
to ask King Herod
about the baby king.

King Herod was mean.

He tried to trick the wise men.

"Find the baby king for me
so I can worship him," he said.

King Herod had a plan.

He wanted to get rid

of Jesus.

The star led the wise men
all the way to Jesus.
They gave Jesus gifts.

An angel told the wise men,
"Do not go back
to King Herod."
So the wise men took
a different road home.

When King Herod found out,
he was very angry.

King Herod yelled,
"Find the boy! I am
the only king!"

Then an angel told Joseph,
"Take your family far away.
You are not safe here."

So Joseph took Mary and
Jesus far, far away.

Jesus grew and grew.
Mary and Joseph loved
Jesus so much.

One day, an angel
said to Joseph,
"It is safe.
Now you can go home."

Joseph, Mary, and Jesus
went back home.
Jesus grew up and told
many people about God's love.